Framework for Leadership

Framework for Leadership

◆

Tools and Resources

Sergio Chiappetta
and
Daron Sandbergh

iUniverse, Inc.
New York Lincoln Shanghai

Framework for Leadership
Tools and Resources

iUniverse, Inc.

For information address:
iUniverse, Inc.
2021 Pine Lake Road, Suite 100
Lincoln, NE 68512
www.iuniverse.com

ISBN: 0-595-33592-6

Printed in the United States of America

Contents

Quotes From The Authors ix

Now It's Time To Build The Organization! xi

Preface xiii

Introduction To Leadership—"The Foundation" 1

Test For Leadership—"Are You Ready?" 9

Vision—"Defining The Future" 11

Decision Making—"Arriving At The Right Decision" 17

Motivation—"Energizing The Workforce" 26

Communication—"Sending The Intended Message" 33

Team Work—"Creating High Performance" 43

Coaching Your Employees For Success—"Developing Key
    Talent" 50

Adaptability—"Dealing With Change" 60

Development—"Growing The Right Talent" 65

Organizational Culture—"Defining The Intangible" 73

Closing Thoughts 79

Index 83

Acknowledgements

Our sincerest thanks to all the colleagues and friends for providing valuable insights, lessons and experiences over the course of the past fifteen years. This culmination of shared knowledge has inspired the vision for "Framework for Leadership."

Special thanks go out to family and friends for their help and support in reviewing and editing our work.

Quotes From The Authors

"An effective leader is someone who is exceptional at influencing and motivating others to do their best for the organization and their customers through achieving results and deliverables."

—Sergio Chiappetta

"Managers manage processes and assets, while leaders lead people. Many organizations do a great job of turning technical experts into good managers, but they fail at creating leaders."

—Daron Sandbergh

Now It's Time To Build The Organization!

Authors Sergio L. Chiappetta and Daron B. Sandbergh have designed a blueprint to effective leadership through the tools and resources identified in, *Framework for Leadership*. The authors present the eight key traits to effective leadership. The book provides models as well as useful exercises leaders can take back to their organization.

The eight key leadership traits are:

- Vision
- Motivation
- Teamwork
- Adaptability
- Decision Making
- Communication
- Coaching
- Development

Testimonials for *Framework for Leadership*

"A wonderful guide and resource which identifies key traits individuals should develop to become a successful leader. Easy to understand concepts and hands-on exercises will work in any organization."

—Michael J. Farrell, Branch Manager, Manpower Professional

"In today's fast paced business, our need to define the roles and responsibilities for all associates will help engage and retain talent. *Framework for Leadership* defines all the aspects of a successful business and the growth from inside out."

—Phyllis Murray, Corporate Director of Human Resources and Safety, Kenosha Beef International and Birchwood Foods, Kenosha, WI.

"*Framework for Leadership* provides a blueprint for maximizing leadership skills. Combining concepts with self-measurement techniques makes the critical skills of leadership available to everyone."

—Mark R. Schubring, Senior Vice President, BayTree National Bank & Trust Company, Lake Forest, IL.

Preface

Sergio Chiappetta

During the formative years of college, my interest in human interactions led me to study sociological behavior and business administration. I combined both disciplines to begin my path in training and development. As I increased my knowledge and became familiar with the needs of corporate America, I began to focus on leadership and answer the questions: What are the essential traits to becoming an effective leader? How do some leaders succeed and others fail? Thus, I began to develop a curriculum for leadership. Through one of my assignments, I was teamed up with a colleague, my coauthor who had the same passion and drive for leadership development. Because of our shared interest, we decided to collaborate on our collective experiences and produce, *Framework for Leadership*.

Daron Sandbergh

From the first time I had "leadership" responsibility as a young sailor I knew that this was a different job than being a technical expert. I recognized this fact over the years as I wound my way through a variety of jobs and positions, always in shock over the widespread lack of preparation that organizations *don't* dedicate to their new supervisors. The adverse effect of a new leader stumbling through goals and objectives, either barking out orders or forgetting to provide any amount of direction, demoralizes his or her employees to a point of horror! In addition, these leaders know that their employees are not as productive as they should be, but they can't figure out what's wrong with their *people*! I know this to be true…I was one of those new leaders stumbling through the dark and stepping on my employees, never realizing that it was dark because I had my eyes shut. I've tried to contribute to this book in an effort to help leaders open their eyes and master some of the fundamentals of leadership.

Our Work

The traditional approach to management (autocratic) involved maintaining absolute control and the use of any means to accomplish desired end results. To continue to maintain that control in order to carry out goals and tasks has serious reprisals.

This book positions eight leadership traits as opposed to the management *techniques* (Theories X and Y) expressed by Douglas McGregor.[1] Both of these theories add immense value to management and leadership aspects for an organization. In theory X, one presumes that the average employee does not want to work and attempts to get out of it or does as little as possible, which is viewed as lazy. These employees have no aspiration, nor do they want to be empowered, and will wait to be directed by the supervisor. This shows a lack of initiative. Even when employees are presented with some of the simplest decisions, they will wait for a leader to make it for them. Theory X employees do not feel that they add value to the organization, nor do they want to. In this theory, employees are not seen as adaptable but viewed as confrontational. Theory X describes that nothing motivates employees to accept challenging assignments, task and goals. The thought here is that employees are malleable, and only work for compensation.

In Theory Y, one presumes that an average employee's profession can be seen as enjoyable and pleasurable, not boring. Employees will take on more responsibilities and challenging assignments rather than just get by. With this approach, greater commitment is created through participative management, which empowers employees. Motivation and energy is robust, hence development for employees becomes essential and crucial. An effective leader's characteristics must include the traditional management traits: controlling, organizing, planning and motivating the employee. Our focus will be the leadership aspect with the key leadership traits identified in this book (supporting Theory Y). This concept applies to a small or large organization. A leader also needs to be accountable for future leaders. A leader cannot allow talent to go unrecognized and unutilized. A leader needs to bring inspiration to the organization as well as the employee. The ideas, values, beliefs and principles apply to all levels of management (formal and informal). Readers will need to self identify themselves in the various roles they fulfill. This role can be found in corporations, institutions, government and non-profit organizations. Large corporations have supervisors, managers and executives, while in small organizations these people are often referred to as front line managers or "top level" managers (or something in between). In government,

---

1.   The Human Side of Enterprise, New York, McGregor-Hill, 1960, Douglas McGregor.

these people are known as supervisors or directors. Even the education system has multiple levels of management (i.e. teachers, principals and superintendents).

All organizations may not have nor require all three levels of leadership (management) or in some organizations leaders my have multiple roles and responsibilities. It's noteworthy to stress that the alignment of individual goals to the organization's goals are fundamental (establishing a clear vision). Prior to creating the vision, the leader is required to understand and know the business. Then the leader can begin with the vision for the organization.

Introduction To
Leadership—"The Foundation"

"Leadership is getting people to work for you when they are not obligated."
—Fred Smith, FedEx

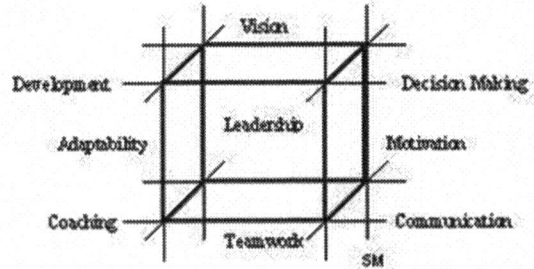

Today's leader needs to model desired behaviors, set direction, inspire employees and possess eight key leadership traits in order to meet the organization's objectives. This chapter opens with the necessary fundamentals of leadership and works towards identifying the eight traits for effectively leading your employees and the organization.

Leadership is not easy nor is it a scientific process. Never the less, leaders can be developed with the right focus. When employees can understand and identify with their leaders, they will support them. In this book, we will supply the tools and resources you need to acquire the behaviors and traits that lead to effective leadership. By providing information and examples, we will stress the importance of several points:

- Set a clear and concise message for your employees. It is critical to communicate to your people where leadership will take the organization. Research shows that employees who understand where the organization is

1

headed are more productive and loyal. Organizations and their people need to understand roles and responsibilities.

- Lead by example so employees know and understand the expectations, values, and norms of the organization. Make sure the example you set is worth following. In any organization, it's crucial for employees to do the appropriate things, especially when leaders are not present.

- Build a relationship and create an alliance with employees. Listen to their innovative ideas to build on the alliance.

- Lead to win. Don't accept the way things are being fulfilled in the organization. If policies and procedures are unjust, make the proper adjustments and changes. By making a difference for the employees, you will build trust and respect among employees.

- Rectify situation in which employees are being treated unfairly.

- Build supportive relationships with your people and lead within your own comfort zone.

- Adopt the key leadership traits. Leadership is a set of skills cultivated over time.

- Develop your employees. Future leaders need to be taught to lead—through experience, training and coaching. Help your employees understand that failures will occur, and let them learn from those failures.

- Have confidence when taking risks; make the right decision for your people and the organization.

- Take a new approach to create a new cultural style by enlightening and empowering your employees.

What do organizations need to do to attract and retain employees? Employees entering the workplace today have different needs and wants from their leaders. Leaders need to pay close attention to these needs and create a workplace with the appropriate values, integrity and character.

Much of leadership entails achieving results through influencing others. Employers today need to give their people the appropriate resources and tools in order to be successful in their roles. The job and responsibility of a leader is to increase productivity of their employees and remove barriers or bottlenecks. Leadership is about bringing people into the process. Allowing employees to contribute to the organization's success will foster employee engagement that increases value and productivity. This gives us the answer to the classic question: "Can one person make a difference in any organization?" We will identify and provide the key leadership traits to assist both new and seasoned leaders in creating those premier organizations. Creative, dedicated, and talented leaders are a scarce resource.

Today's business environment demands that all managers effectively display both leadership and management skills. Leaders need to listen to their people to find out what their needs encompass. This book will concentrate on the importance of the leadership aspect. It is designed to assist in developing effective leaders. Ultimate success is realized by developing leaders who will build trusting relationships with employees while leading the organization to the achievement of its vision and goals.

A critical role of a leader is to establish a relationship with employees and create an environment that will help inspire innovation. A leader must always be on the lookout for talent and ideas throughout their organization. Employees in today's workplace want to be considered valuable intellectual assets. They want their organization to care about their future development, opportunities, and other stability needs. Leaders influence their people through thoughts, decisions and behaviors that ultimately affect (change) their people and the organization's long-term viability and profitability. Leaders need to be flexible. The amount of support, guidance and direction each employee needs will vary.

Organizations need to be able to generate the deliverables and results for their clients, customers, and their employees as well as social responsibility for their surrounding communities.

We must constantly remind ourselves that organizations are only as effective as the people within the organization. Leaders and their organizations need to think outside the box, creating incentives and opportunities for both professional growth and development.

Employees need to feel that their job is important and meaningful to their organization. Employees want to know that their ideas and thoughts matter. A leader's role involves connecting employees to the organization. It's a leader's responsibility to identify what challenges an employee, and continuously motivate employees with challenging assignments. Take responsibility to make sure employees are the right fit for their role or job function.

In this book we stress the need to meet with your employees regularly. A leader should be able to sense potential problems before talented employees exit. Through on-going communication, they will feel connected to the organization, and be able to influence outcomes.

Management vs. Leadership Behavior Identifier

Directions: check one of the paired statements that you can closely relate to on the job.

	Statements	Check One
1.	a. My role mainly consists of budgeting. b. My role is to provide empowerment / guidance in the annual budgeting process.	
2.	a. My responsibilities include hiring and staffing for my department. b. I seek input in selection process when staffing my department.	
3.	a. I hold annual performance reviews with all direct reports. b. I oversee the performance review process and encourage my direct reports to provide contribution for employee(s) assessment.	
4.	a. I am responsible for controlling all aspects of decision making for my department. b. I empower employee(s) to make the right choices.	
5.	a. I establish all goals for this organization. b. Employees are expected to participate in the goal setting process.	
6.	a. I maintain all input for performance related issues of my staff. b. I act as a sounding board for issues as they arise.	
7.	a. I establish and maintain all work schedules. b. We offer flexibility in our organization.	
8.	a. I create next year's budget based on last year's numbers. b. Team identifies and projects employee needs for the year.	
9.	a. I select all promotional opportunities for my area. b. We have a growth plan process in place.	
10.	a. I rely on my technical expertise. b. I surround myself with the appropriate individuals.	

For each "A" response selected, you have indicated a more technical "managerial" behavior, while the "B" responses indicate what we have defined as "effective leadership" behaviors.

> *"Managers do things right. Leaders do the right things."*
>
> —*Warren Bennis and Burt Nanus*

The New Leadership Model

We have built a model that differentiates "Manager" responsibilities (planning, organizing, controlling, hiring & staffing, budgeting and administration) from those of a "Leader". These include establishing a vision, communication, teamwork, motivating, developing, empowering and enlightening. Our model looks at the basics of leadership and provides the blueprint, made up of the combination of essential traits to create an effective leader. Thinking out of the box and going outside the lines allows organizations to continue success. The lines outside the box link today's problems to new solutions. We need to align the organization and employee's needs to reach the organization's vision. Empowering employees to generate ideas, concepts, and solutions will allow organizations to continue their competitiveness in the future. We need to train and develop our key assets, leaders and employees. Organizations need to offer the appropriate training approaches to deliver the right solutions. The T.E.A.M.WORKS[SM] framework demonstrates and signifies creativity and innovation in developing the organization and it's talent. (T.E.A.M.WORKS[SM] is a talent development firm focusing on growth and maximization of leadership talent).

The Framework

Research has identified more than 300 leadership traits. Based on our experience within the field of talent development, we have narrowed it down to eight key traits, which tend to be the most visibly observed behaviors.

We recommend that you start with *Vision* when building the skills of an effective leader. A leader needs to be able to convey and communicate the vision first and foremost. The leader needs to make sure that the vision is aligned with the business objectives and goals. The remainder of the traits can be developed in any order. After discussing each leadership trait, we list associated key behaviors.

Trait #1 Vision:

A leader needs to make sure that everyone in the organization understands the team's purpose. Every employee in the organization needs to know and understand their individual role and how that role fits in with the overall vision. This will assist the leader to focus and provide direction.

Trait #2 Decision Making:

Leaders need to effectively deal with ethical dilemmas and have integrity in the workplace. It is critical to define the expectations and structure for employees. Employees need to evaluate and choose the appropriate choices.

Trait #3 Motivation:

Motivation has become a powerful avenue for today's leader. One needs to personalize praise when you catch employees doing things right. In return, a leader establishes a positive relationship and creates a role model for others in the organization to follow.

Empowerment: A leader needs to provide an environment that empowers and enlightens employees. This starts with giving employees the time and opportunities they need to experience new challenges and responsibilities. The starting point is to build a relationship with their employees by developing and ensuring accountability and ownership.

Attitude: Attitude is a matter of choice, and a positive attitude is indispensable. Give employees meaningful work to assist in developing the right attitude for the organization. Understand what holds meaning for each individual.

Trait #4 Communication:

Today's leaders need to be clear and concise in their communication. Once achieved, it improves relationships. It allows one to build effective alliances, which in return enhances organizational effectiveness.

Set Clear Goals and Expectations: This behavior gives employees the right tools to perform their job. Tactful communication develops employees for growth opportunities and creates a work environment in which they can thrive.

Trait #5 Teamwork:

A leader is responsible for providing a structure that encourages a sense of involvement within the organization. Organizations today are more complex. This complexity and growing competition creates a need for creating high-quality solutions, which is only possible when you build high performing teams.

Trait #6 Coaching:

The coach provides performance feedback that is work-related and speaks to abilities, skills and willingness to achieve personal and organizational goals.

Trait #7 Adaptability:

A leader becomes meaningful to the organization when they figure out how to achieve the desired outcomes. Once accomplished, the leader needs to influence the performance of others and lead others through change.

Innovation: Being an effective leader means one is looking for alternative solutions. This means a leader needs to welcome opinions and ideas and that they are valued in their contributions to the organization. A leader needs to encourage and ask for input.

Trait #8 Development:

Learning is a lifelong process. Employees are only ready when they are willing to be developed. Employees develop best when they perform or practice. Giving employees the opportunity to practice in a safe environment builds confidence.

Leaders need to value thinking. We stress the importance for leaders to ask themselves what their employees are capable of and provide them with the resources. Leadership needs to go in every direction, not just from the top down. The difference between a leader and an *effective leader* is the ability to pick themselves up after they have fallen.

Test For Leadership—"Are You Ready?"

"A leader has the vision and conviction that a dream can be achieved. He inspires the power and energy to get it done."

—*Ralph Lauren*

Self Examination/Self Check

As a leader, ask yourself if you posses these successful behaviors and traits of an effective leader?

- Provide timely feedback
- Coach
- Communicate effectively
- Listens
- Offer meaningful work
- Provide praise
- Support employees
- Set mutual expectations

Take former Mayor Rudi Guiliani as an example. In a time of crisis (September 11, 2001) Mayor Guiliani stepped up as an effective leader. He had a vision, and he established communications with the community as well as the world. He energized the citizens, who came forward to provide labor and financial assistance (teamwork). The mayor and the community adapted quickly in the ever-changing environment. He was decisive in this moment of crisis, and to the public eye, was unwavering. Rudi listened to the needs of those in his city, supported those who had volunteered, and praised the heroes of the moment.

Remember organizations are only as good as the people within the organizations. In order to keep top performers, organizations need to *think out of the box* and create incentives such as opportunities for professional growth and development. We have identified eight traits that leaders need to incorporate in order to build a high performance organization with an empowered culture. Leaders need to make it clear to employees that these initiatives are supported:

- Vision (organization and team purpose)
- Decision Making (decisiveness, conviction and execution)
- Motivation (positive attitudes and energizing the workforce)
- Communication (timely, clear and concise)
- Teamwork (the foundation and infrastructure)
- Coaching (developing and challenging talent)
- Adaptability (flexible in changing times)
- Development (provide opportunity and grow key talent)

Vision—"Defining The Future"

"You can deal with the future more clearly if you don't focus on the next week."

—John Templeton, Founder of Templeton Funds

Test Your Knowledge: What Is Vision?

- Do your employees/team members know where you are going?

- Do *you* know where you are going?

- Can you picture the future?

- Do your values mirror the organization's values?

- Do you know the purpose of your organization?

In the process of developing effective leadership, the framework begins with the vision. Architects don't start designing without a vision and you can't start building your organization without a clear vision. This chapter will describe why a clear vision is crucial, and how to design the path to success.

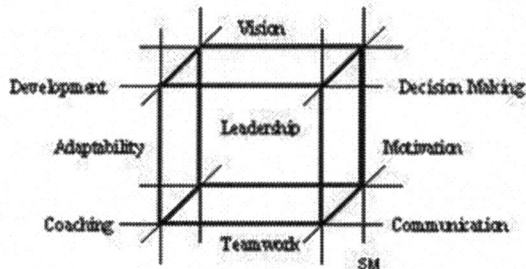

Effective leaders are adept at communicating the future vision, and the strategies necessary to get "there". Spending time up front defining your vision makes the job of communication easier and clearer.

Plotting Your Course

1. Develop and communicate the vision of future performance and practice:

    *   Brainstorm and identify what your team's ideal picture of the organization would look like, without constraints such as money, head count, and equipment. Develop the picture of the future as if you were creating the organization from scratch, and there were no limits.

    *   Work with your team to build a joint vision, while driving and communicating your personal vision.

2. Define key success factors to obtain future vision:

    *   Understand your organization and what it takes to succeed. Examine the roadblocks, from cultural and operational perspectives.

3. Analyze "current trends" that impact the organization as of today:

    *   What is changing within the organization? How will this impact your efforts and your team? Are you prepared for the future?

4. Understand the current state:

    *   Clearly define your current organization, using actionable phrases.

5. Identify the Gap. Define underlying contradictions between the current state and the future vision. Define the causes, in terms of both depth and breadth, of the current state:

- Define the gap in terms of what needs to be done or what needs to happen.

6. Compare the identified gaps with the current and projected business issues:

    - Double back and ensure that your "actions" identified are not going to conflict with the direction the organization is taking.

7. Develop strategies and associated metrics to meet the key success factors. Monitor performance:

    - Define the metrics…how will you know you are there? You must have clearly defined metrics for each action, or you may become trapped in work with no outcome! Once you understand where you are going, define action steps with deadlines.

"Usually if everybody is going in one direction, it's wrong."

—Hank Greenberg

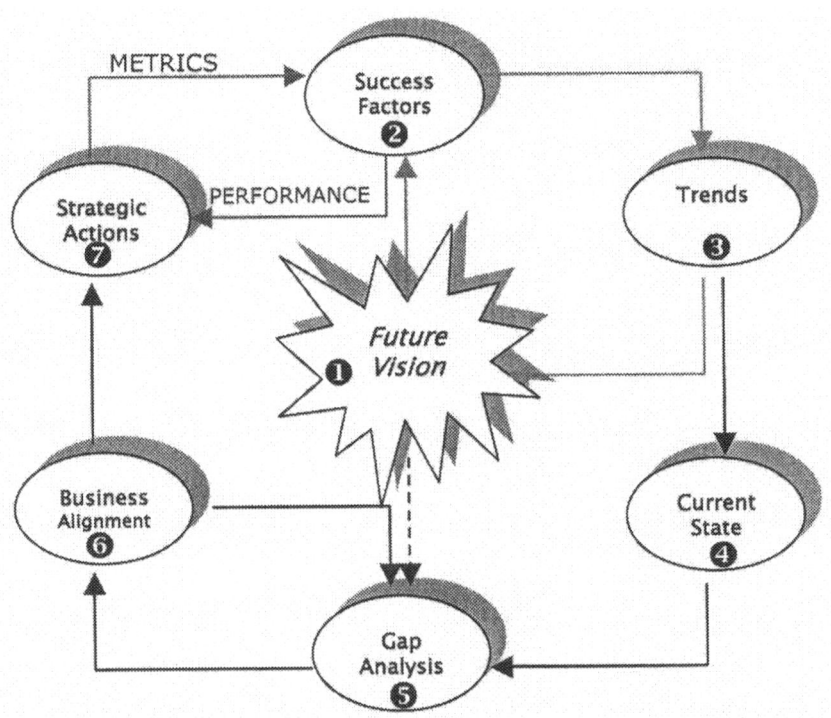

Your Point Of View

The vision you create is a subjective and moving target. Consider this exercise:

1. Find a distant object

2. Cover your right eye with your right hand, and point to the object with your left hand.

3. Now, without moving your pointing hand, move your right hand over your left eye.

4. What happened to the object? If you are like most people, the object shifted.

We often forget that our employees don't have the same background information as you do. You have to work with your employees and get them involved in defining the vision to increase understanding.

> *"We know only two things about the future: It cannot be known, and it will be different from what exists now and from what we now expect."*
>
> —*Peter Drucker, Business Philosopher and Author*

Developing a Mission Statement

Articulates why organizations exist:

- Primary justification for existence

- Service or product lines

- Customer

- Products and services provided

- How products and services will be provided

- Steps to create the mission statement:

  - Brainstorm key components

  - Determine what we worry about every day (customers, quality, employee cost)

  - Determine why we exist

- Develop a draft statement
- Discuss
- Finalize

Developing a Vision Statement

A Vision Statement has a long-term focus and describes the organization in its ideal state. It provides clear goals concerning aspects such as:

- Market share

- Profitability

- Impact on competition

- Impact on employees

- Impact on customers

- Steps to create a vision statement:

  - Work one component at a time
  - Determine the defining characteristics, does it instill passion, communicate a clear, visual image, align with the future external market
  - Develop a draft statement
  - Discuss
  - Finalize

KEY BEHAVIORS
"Vision"

- Directional, realistic

- Strategic thinker, planner

- Organized

- Trustworthy, credible

- Clear and concise communication

- Awareness of trends (internal/external)

- Risk taker (calculated)

Decision Making—"Arriving At The Right Decision"

"One of the biggest things I've learned is I don't always need to be right."
—*Jeffrey B. Swartz, Timberland*

Test Your Knowledge: What Makes A Good Choice?

- Do you have a process to make decisions?

- How do you know when to make a decision?

- How do you communicate your decisions and their impact?

- Do you second-guess your decisions?

- Who contributes to the decision-making process?

A critical behavior of any effective leader is the ability to make timely and informed decisions. In this chapter, we provide the process and steps to assist you in arriving at the right options for your organization.

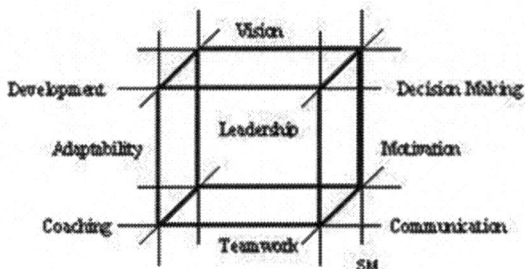

Organizations need to realize that leaders come and go. We must recognize past leaders including their accomplishments and failures. This will assist new leaders in making future decisions without repeating mistakes. How does an employee get direction? Making decisions as a leader requires confidence, competence and patience in your role. How crucial is it to make the right decision? How do you know if the decision was the right one? How do you evaluate the process? How does your decision affect the organization and others? You need to be able to reflect on your decision.

When decisions fail, leaders need to be able to acknowledge the mistake, rectify the situation, learn and not repeat the mistake.

Another tool available to assist leaders and their organizations in the decision making process is the *SWOT Analysis*.

SWOT—This tool allows for analysis of your own internal potential, and to set that in relation to what you know about the future situation.

Strengths:
What is the organization good at?
Identify the pool of talent.

Weaknesses:
Are there negative perceptions of the organization?
Identify your talent gaps.

Opportunities:
What is happening that could help us?
Are there opportunities we could take advantage of?

Threats:
What circumstances could hurt us?
What don't we know?

Leaders and their employees need to take accountability and responsibility for their actions and decisions or lack there of. This sense of ownership needs to be embedded in all organizations that not only hope to survive, but succeed. Anticipating what would happen is a crucial component in effective leadership and decision-making. Food for thought: If I'm aware that an inappropriate action has taken place, what will I do? The decision making process involves understanding of goals and objectives when making decisions. This provides a strong foundation for all decision-making. Prior to making a decision, the decision making process needs to allow creative thinking, allowing free flow of many possible options. We stress the importance of integrating many of the individual perspectives that may effect the decision. Reaching consensus is one of the most widely used decision making techniques used by corporations and organizations. This allows for open discussion of all alternative options and encourages involvement from everyone, which will result in commitment from all parties.

Environmental Scan—This tool is useful in developing a shared understanding of the internal and external factors that influence the organization.

Instructions

1. Define the organization to be scanned.

2. Identify factors that influence the situation such as:

   • Internal (practices, policies, culture)

   • External (clients, vendors)

3. Break into groups to discuss the effects of these factors.

Example:

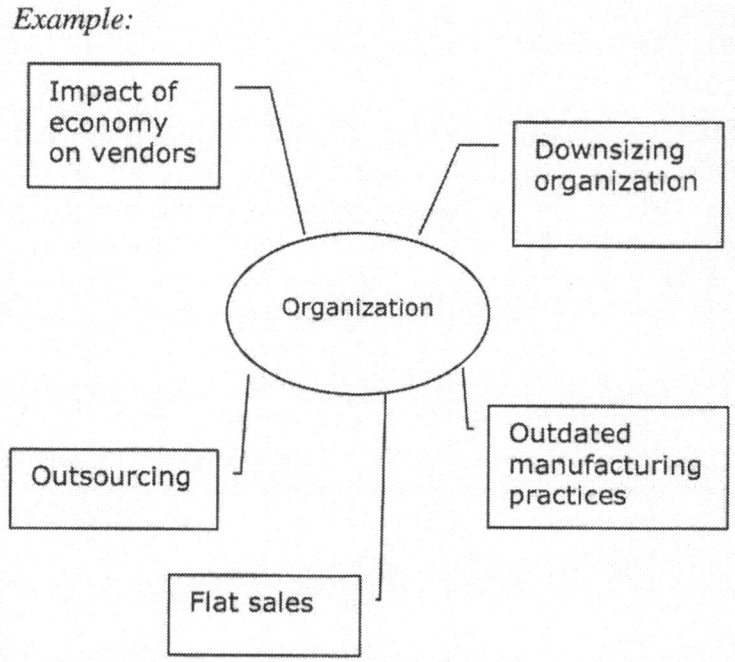

The decisions we make as leaders should not have negative consequences to others. As an organization responsible to its employees as well as society, corporations and leaders are required to be socially responsible and deal with ethical dilemmas appropriately. All leaders and their employees have personal values and life experiences that influence their decision making process. Leaders need to acknowledge and be aware of their own judgments when making these decisions.

A critical element of decision-making is the concept of ethics. A poor decision can result in scandal, loss of market share, lower profits and damaged credibility. Values, beliefs and assumptions must be in line with the decisions you make. Leaders must always act with integrity.

The Decision Case Study

The example we will share is the tool and process that a car manufacturer (to be left unnamed) used to make their decision on whether or not to fix each vehicle's fuel tank on a popular model.

Crash tests had revealed a serious defect in the fuel tank. In crashes over 25 mph, the fuel tank always ruptured. The company had conducted a cost benefit analysis of human life. To correct this defect, it would have required changing and straightening the design. According to estimates, the unsafe tanks would cause 180 burn deaths, 180 serious burn injuries, and 2100 burned vehicles each year. Based on a formula and calculation they estimated they would pay $200,000 per death, $67,000 per injury and $700 per vehicle for a total of $49.5 million. This was seen as less expensive than the cost of recalling and repairing the vehicles.

As it turns out, the cost of lives and injuries ran higher than the company had estimated (analysts have speculated that the actual cost of repair would have been less than $10.00 per vehicle).

Was this the right decision to make? Would this decision have been made today? What were the hindrances in this decision making process (was it greed or cost). What would today's effective leader do?

*Source: Order, Law, and Crime: An Introduction to Criminology by Raymond J. Michalowski published January 1st, 1985.

Effective Decision Making Process

State Reason Or Purpose

Establish a clear and mutual understanding to provide direction or goal. Understanding the end goal will prevent wasted resources.

Brainstorm Alternatives And Options

Generate a variety (depth and breadth) of tactics to address the issue. Keep all ideas intact until next step. Prevent from dismissing ideas quickly.

Discuss Options And Evaluate With The Team

Review and discuss the options with the employees impacted by the decision. Give voice to all those involved.

Select Best Alternative

Involve and discuss options with employees. You, as a leader, must select the best alternative.

Design The Plan

Clearly document the communication plan including target audience and impacted employees, dates and accountabilities. Some avenues may include: employee meetings, technology, posters, department level meetings or mail as appropriate. Keep in mind all employees may not have equal access to all forms of media. This design must also include defined mechanisms to measure successful implementation.

Communicate Decision

Publicize relevant aspect of the decision, its purpose and impact. Make sure you publish or announce to all employees in your organization.

Execute Decision

Implement the decision including required training, updating of policies, creation of job aides, and other tools. Without successful execution and creation of these supporting tools, the decision will not become a part of the organization's culture.

Evaluate The Effectiveness Of The Decision

Measure and communicate progress and results. We recommend conducting annual climate surveys of your organization to check for the success of the implementation. Part of this process may include employee focus groups and/or online questionnaires.

Effective Decision Making Process

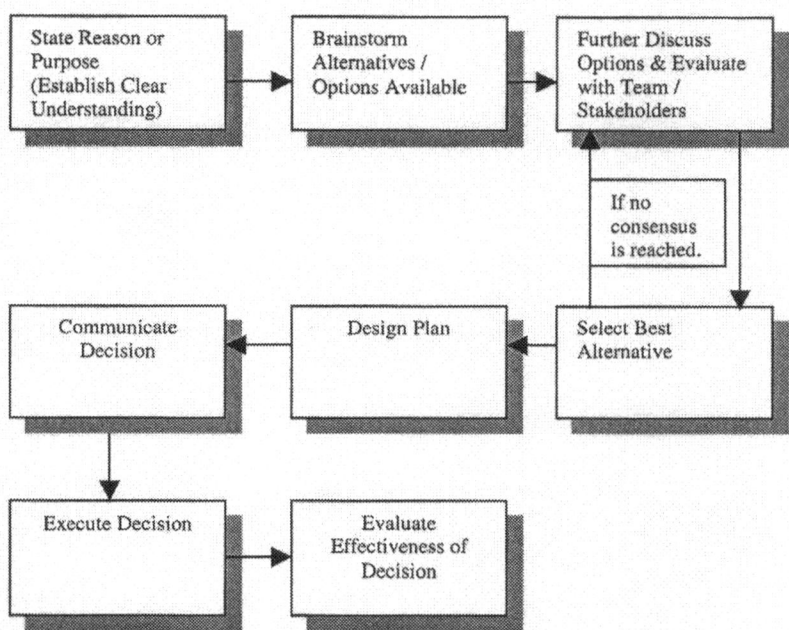

Setting Priorities

Many times leaders find that their organization has taken on responsibilities that do not align with their vision. In such cases, it becomes necessary to determine what is important, or what activities are needed to achieve organizational goals.

The following decision making process allows you to understand your business and which daily activities support your business objectives.

Case Study: Setting Priorities

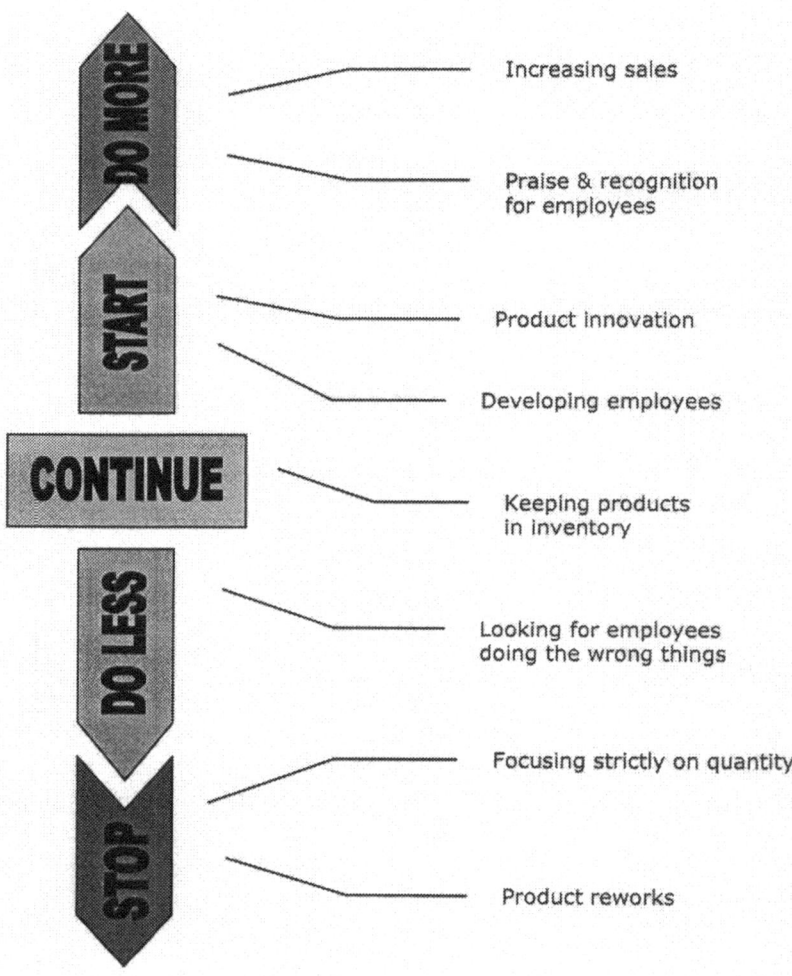

Increasing sales

Praise & recognition
for employees

Product innovation

Developing employees

Keeping products
in inventory

Looking for employees
doing the wrong things

Focusing strictly on quantity

Product reworks

KEY BEHAVIORS
"Decision Making"

- Apply lessons learned

- Timely

- Proactive

- Logical thinker, informed decisions

- Confident

- Goal oriented vs. "trendy"

- Balance of fact and feeling

- Sense of ethics

Motivation—"Energizing The Workforce"

"The true motivation for employees is the spirit of cooperation that comes with a shared vision."

—Greg Bustic, Tracey-Lock Public Relations

Test Your Knowledge: What Is Motivation?

- What motivates your employees?

- Are dollars the only motivator that employees want?

- How regularly do you praise your employees for a "job well done"?

- Is the best solution for dealing with unmotivated employees to "let them go?"

- Are your employees highly energized and passionate about their organization?

Leaders need to transform their employees through relationship building and reward their employees for a job well done. In order for organizations to raise the bar, leaders need to establish a positive and creative work environment so employees can add value to the overall goal of the organization. What are the key ingredients in motivating employees?

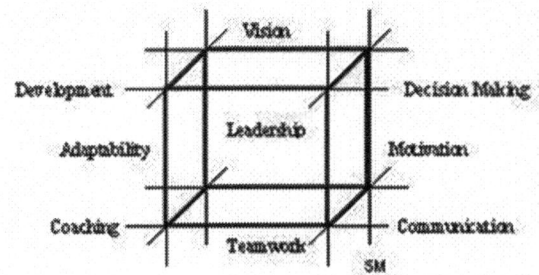

A question that effective leaders will have to answer: "How do you get employees to perform well and retain them?" Start with building a trusting environment, building that two-way communication, and by giving employees meaningful work. To build trust takes time, so leaders need to commit time to each employee (there are no shortcuts). Once leaders establish a proven track record with employees, they will get the buy-in and consequential payoff.

We need to spend less time on ineffective behavior. There's a need to allow employees to learn from their mistakes because it's the right thing to do. (Keep in mind we need to recognize it, deal with it and then move on).

It's loud and clear that certain organizations do a mediocre job of recognizing employee contributions. We need to remind ourselves that our people are the heart of the organization. Survey after survey employees have indicated performance motivators-such as approach, understanding, attitude, interesting work and communication.

Here are some motivating factors:

- Job enrichment, which includes changes in task, increasing responsibility, personal achievements, constructive feedback and development.
- Employee's contributions need to be value-added to the organization.
- The opportunity for advancement keeps employees motivated.
- Good performance needs to be followed with positive reinforcement by their leaders.
- Increasing involvement and input in the process, which adds value to the bottom line.

A retention-focused leader develops people for growth opportunities, creates a work environment that they love, has a leadership style that empowers and enlightens employees and encourages employees to keep up the good work or provides the appropriate feedback to get back on track.

Some motivational problems may be due to not finding the right fit for the employee. When moving an employee to another position, organizational problems may occur—the employee may find the new position dull or uninspiring, causing morale to worsen regardless of the amount of training the employee is given.

Effective leaders need to answer these questions associated around what motivates employees. What does it take to motivate your workplace? How does an effective leader gain commitment and buy-in from the employee?

What Stimulates Employee's To Continue To Be Productive On The Job?

- Praise from the boss

- Recognition

- Flexibility on the job

- Development opportunities

- Casual clothing

- Working from home

- Pay/Increases

- Award celebrations

- Joining a team

- Believe in what organization does

- Promotion

- Challenge assignments

- Paid meals

• Celebrate work anniversaries

Keep in mind that employee want to work hard and receive recognition from their leaders.

Directions:

Complete the following instrument based on your perception of the organization. Low scores may indicate morale issues, potential employees rebelling, or no structure or systems in place for rewards and recognition programs. High scores indicate infrastructure is in place, employees feel that their contributions add value to the organization.

Measuring Motivation

Directions: Rate the factors of each item using the following scale. Evaluate the current work environment. How much of the factors listed below currently exist in the present organization.

Rewards and Recognition

Non-existent		Demonstrated		Established
1	2	3	4	5

Job Security

Non-existent		Demonstrated		Established
1	2	3	4	5

Value-Added Work

Non-existent		Demonstrated		Established
1	2	3	4	5

Clear Direction

Non-existent		Demonstrated		Established
1	2	3	4	5

Development and Promotional Opportunities

Non-existent		Demonstrated		Established
1	2	3	4	5

Sense of Belonging

Non-existent		Demonstrated		Established
1	2	3	4	5

What the Company Stands For

Non-existent		Demonstrated		Established
1	2	3	4	5

A Vision

Non-existent		Demonstrated		Established
1	2	3	4	5

The Top Five Motivating Techniques:

1. The leader personally congratulates employees when they do a good job.

2. The leader writes personal notes about good performance.

3. The organization uses performance as the basis for promotion.

4. The leader properly recognizes employees for good performance.

5. The leader holds morale-building meetings to celebrate success.

Guidelines To Track A Reward And Recognition Program For Your Organization

Programs should reflect the organization's values and business strategy, employees should participate in development, involve cash and/or non-cash rewards and should be highly public for employees that so desire.

> *"A workplace that has achieved motivation will create the premier organization that stakeholders want and the high performing teams that employees require to achieve optimal productivity."*
>
> *—Sergio Chiappetta*

What Do Employees Want From Their Workplace?

Directions: Hand out exercise during a staff meeting or offsite session. Based on your response place a check in the appropriate box.

1. Which is more important	Enthusiasm or Education	
2. Would rather receive	Cash or Non-cash gift	
3. Increase performance from employees by	Raise or Training	
4. Which is more inspirational	Trusted or Appreciated	
5. Which is more important	Creativity Or Job Title	
6. Receiving praise from	Boss or Colleagues	
7. Need additional responsibilities	Challenge or Increase Pay	
8. Having lunch with	Senior Management or Family	
9. The need for	Freedom or Structure	
10. Concerns with	Benefits or Job Security	

KEY BEHAVIORS
"Motivation"

- Hold employees accountable

- Understand and know your people

- Vision driven—for a reason

- Recognizes potential in employees

- Lead by example

- Give credit when credit is due

- Demonstrate mutual respect

Communication—"Sending The Intended Message"

"Today, a great CEO must be a great communicator."

—*Fred Raines*

Test Your Knowledge: What Is Communication?

- Is your organization utilizing the best communication channels to meet the business objectives? How do you know?

- Do your employees receive messages in the manner in which you intend?

- In your organization, do employees clearly understand expectations?

- How do you address inadequate communication?

- Do stakeholders create alliances to meet strategic business objectives?

- How effective are your work teams?

In this chapter we will address the question "Why do some leaders find it difficult to communicate with their employees?" In order for most of us to be able to function on a daily basis, communication is a fundamental need.

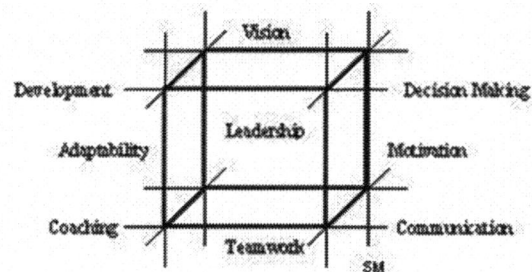

In some cases leaders feel rushed. They don't take the necessary time to communicate to their organizations and employees. A key issue in corporate America today is the lack of communication. This section will help leaders address these communication problems. Effective communication requires trust, cooperation and the ability to build a rapport with others to continue organizational success. Most of us can learn more about better communication. We have provided a model that will speak to effective communication, which will create equally desired outcomes. In order to create effective communication, there needs to be a connection between relationships and goals.

Communication breakdown occurs when information and resources are not shared with the organization and its' employees. Oftentimes communications are only partially shared which creates confusion and rumors. Improving communication in the workplace is the most important investment leaders can make for the organization and the employee. A leader's role is to eliminate communication problems before any real issues arise.

Communication excellence requirements include timely messages, constant two-way communication and the ability to choose the right words. Basic communication is designed to transmit information to additional individuals who need information to move forward. This requires the need to be open in order to create an effective team environment. Communication can be established by the use of words and how we express ourselves through body language and facial expressions.

Non-Verbal Indicators

The body—Not interested if leans backward or positions farther away.
The arms—Not receptive if arms are crossed.

The face and head—Untrustworthy if avoids eye contact.
The hands—Negative if palms are down. Nervous and lack confidence if self touching gestures.
The legs—Uncooperative and untrustworthy if legs are crossed.
Frown—Doubt or deep thought.
Stare—Challenge or disagreement.
The Blank Look—Disbelief or "Had Enough"

Some leaders and employees do not really listen. Oftentimes they are just waiting to speak. Interactive listening is a crucial component to the communication process. Typically, this is not a skill that is taught or gets practiced. It is important to listen intently while the other person talks, and focus on understanding the employee's point of view. This demonstrates to the employee that you care as a leader. By listening intently a leader can better prepare a response when the intended message is received. Ultimately, better listeners become key individuals for High Performance Teams and develop a deeper understanding for employee needs.

Communication Mode

Conversation

- Personal and confidential
- Difficult questions can be asked
- Can be intimidating
- Time consuming
- Can check for understanding
- Deliver negative messages
- Inconsistent from person to person (one on one)

All Employee Meetings

- Everyone hears the same message
- Learn & build ideas from others
- Questions can be asked
- Difficult to schedule (number of attendees)

- Discussions can occur
- Difficult to run on a schedule basis
- Not all may be able to attend

Email

- Create anytime
- Volume disbursement
- Details & specifics can be included
- Retain for future
- Time consuming
- Forward to wrong individual
- Receipts may or may not be read

Voice Mail

- Employees tend to respond within 24 hours
- Privacy
- Access from anywhere
- Personal
- Some dislike
- Not detailed enough for some
- Usually not stored for long time period

Leaders need to understand varying expectations of diverse cultures. Periods of silence are completely acceptable during conversation for many cultures.

Communication Assessment

Directions: Use the following scale to rate your communication skills:

1 = Never   2 = Occasionally   3 = Usually 4 = Often   5 = Always

Focus on one individual as you are completing this exercise.

Behavior				
You share information often				
You find it necessary to hold back information				
Your goals are unique to yourself				
Your goals are shared by others				
You feel connected to your organization				
You see things differently from your organization				
You identify with your immediate work group				
You are detached from your team				
You solicit ideas from your team members				
You tend to run with your own ideas				
You tend to experience many "water cooler" discussions with your team.				

	I	II	III	IV
Your conversations are value-added	▬	▬	▬	
You freely voice your objections	▬		▬	▬
You constructively address organizational short-falls	▬	▬		▬
You rely on others to do their share	▬	▬		▬
You are more productive working on your own		▬	▬	▬
There are certain people who you refuse to work with	▬		▬	▬
You enjoy working with anyone in the organization	▬	▬	▬	
You rely on the grapevine for information	▬		▬	▬
You rely on verified information	▬		▬	▬
Total of each column:				
Quadrant	I	II	III	IV

Communication Effectiveness: Relationships vs. Goals

Successful organizational communication is the output of two axes.

Positive work relationships are a major factor in defining how well an organization and individuals are able to communicate. Relationships are determined by the amount of trust and cooperation individuals share with each other.

Commonality of goals, objectives, direction or vision is the second axis leading to effective communication.

Communication Effectiveness: The Model

"Shared Goals" "Connected" "Associated" +	"Distrust" "Lacking Teamwork" "Storming"	"Effective" "Dynamic"
Goals	"Protective" "Secretive" "Possessive"	"Approachable" "Lacking Commitment"
"Personal Goals" "Disconnected" "Disengaged" −		

"Detrimental" "Damaging" "Negative"   Relationship   "Productive" "Hi Performing"

Goals that are intertwined with one another, or interdependent, force the organization to communicate if the goals are to be met. When goals are fragmented, there is little reason to communicate.

Other factors that lead to successful relationships are: attitude, mutual respect, integrity, motivation, effective alliances and individual networks.

Information Is Power!

When a negative relationship exists between individuals who have no common goals, or competing goals, employees involved tend to become protective, secretive and possessive about the information they hold. In extreme situations, efforts to sabotage one another may occur, destroying productivity and profit.

False pretense that security lies in keeping secrets, and that power can be gained in keeping others in the dark sabotages effective communication. For example, the thought, *"If I do better on 'my' goal than my 'opponent' does on their goal, I will win!" is counter-productive.* This archaic thinking stifles valuable communication flow and hinders achievement.

The consequence is that, employees will never share goals and/or be in line to meet organizational objectives due to a defensive relationship with co-workers.

One-Sided Communication

By creating shared goals, people are forced to work more closely together to accomplish their tasks, but this alone will not drive effective communication. Productive relationships fail to exist, leading to one-sided communication. The amount of information flow is limited by an atmosphere of distrust. Employees tend to hold back, seeking the "advantage". The unknown tends to breed fear and suspicion.

There is minimal collaboration, however there is lack of complete cooperation.

Missing Link

Idle chitchat brought out by a positive relationship does not lend to value added, goal oriented communication. Lack of common objectives hinders performance-enhancing communication, and creates a wider communication gap. Communications tend to create an unproductive work environment, fostering complaints and gripes. Low morale drives employees to communicate about non-business topics such as their recent golf score.

An effective leader will find what motivates employees and then provide aligned direction, guidance and purpose through a sense of belonging for the employee as well as tying them to the organization, vision and organizational objectives. Point being, the employees *need* to see the connection.

Even though tasks are being completed and deadlines met, the concern is that the potential of the employees does not equal the highest level of productivity.

Winning Communication

Positive relationships which foster higher levels of trust, combined with common goals, leads to shared information, meaningful dialogue and add value to the organization. A sense of belonging exists due to the established relationships and goal accomplishment. All parties willingly share pertinent information at the appropriate time, leading to winning communication. Winning teams successfully practice winning communication!

A sense of belonging from cooperation to mutual respect allows employees to play on the same team.

KEY BEHAVIORS
"Communication"

- Accurate

- Clear and concise

- Timely

- Demonstrates effective listening skills

- Understand intended message

- Professional

- Deliver positive & negative messages

Team Work—"Creating High Performance"

"Great teams are not hierarchical or autocratic they tap each members creative potential."

—*Fast Company*

Test Your Knowledge: What Is A Team?

- Would your team be more productive if it had five of you?

- Are brainstorming and other "day-dream" activities value-added to team productivity?

- Do teams belong in business organizations, or should they be banished to the sports fields?

- Are teams valuable since your leaders and managers have all the answers?

- Is there a benefit in teams, since one person can move more quickly?

Transforming your staff into high performing teams will happen when people share a common direction and a sense of commitment. This chapter will discuss how organizations transform their employees into team players.

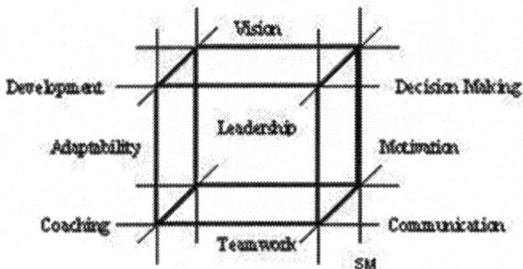

How do you harness the expertise of your organization? The answer—*teamwork*!

The goal of all leaders and organizations is to transform their staff into a high performing team. The purpose of this chapter is to demonstrate that teams outperform individuals working alone. We will demonstrate the need to build high performance teams. Organizations today are more complex and competitive. Through teamwork you achieve greater productivity, more effective use of resources and better problem solving success. The chapter will discuss the basics of teamwork and the fundamentals of team dynamics.

The need for effective leadership comes from a supportive and coaching leadership style, which allows individuals to make choices for themselves and to be directly involved in the decision-making process. Teams are becoming essential for effective decision-making.

There's no doubt that teams make a difference in today's workplace. Teams rule when: employees understand individual and team objectives as well as the purpose of their role. Employees have to comprehend the impact that their contribution makes to the overall organization and how their participation affects the final outcome. In order to see this impact, the overall organization requires effective communication by leadership. High performance requires involvement from all team members. You as a leader need to be flexible to allow changes within the objectives of the overall outcome. We also want to make it clear that teams are not the solution to every problem an organization may have. The team's success is contingent upon how well a leader creates a common direction and sense of commitment for the employee in order to achieve excellence and high performance that organizations require. Organizations entail the use of teams for reducing lead times, cycle times and restructuring organizations, which in turn provides customers with the product or service.

We have identified the following *Team Life Styles*: the **first stage** is the *Introduction of Team Members*. (You may be familiar with Bruce Tuckman's simple four stage team development model.) At this stage, there is excitement and anticipation; members become acquainted. Information is necessary in order to get started. The **second stage** is *Commotion and Confusion (C^2)*. At this stage there is resistance, attitude changes and arguing among the team members begins. The **third stage** is called *Gaining Momentum*. The team is getting use to one another. The team members start assisting each other, which leads to mutual trust and eliminates the competitiveness. Team members learn to work together more effectively. The **fourth stage** we call *High Performance*. Every team member accepts each other's strengths and weaknesses. There is satisfaction of the team's progress and bonding among the team members. Successful teams have a variety of *team player styles*. Most of us have a natural or predominant style. Leaders and organizations need to take advantage of those differences. The styles we have identified are as follows: **Technical**: task orientated member of the team. Brings skills and stability to the team. **Executor**: focuses on the big picture. Resists dealing with specifics. **Amiable:** people person. Looks for the human relations in a group process. **Motivator:** enthusiastic, optimistic, promoter and outspoken. This person brings high energy to the team.

"Vee Formation"
Goose Story

When you see geese flying south along a Vee formation, there's synergy to why they do. As the birds flap their wings, it creates uplift for the bird immediately following. The whole flock improves their flying range by 71 percent than if each bird flew on its own. If a bird falls out of formation, it feels the resistance of trying to fly solo—there's a need to take advantage of the flying power. The lead goose role is demanding. When it comes to leadership for the flock, the lead position gets rotated back in the wing and another goose flies lead position. When the geese make "noise", the honking from behind is to motivate those in front to keep their pace. If a goose gets wounded and falls out of the Vee Formation, two geese fall out with the injured goose and follow him down to protect him. The two geese stay with him until the wounded goose is able to fly or until he is dead and the remaining two try to catch another formation.

—Author Unknown

"To lead the people walk behind them."

—*Lao-TZU*

TEAM PLAYER STYLES

Directions: Circle one word/phrase in each row that best describes you. Then tally the number of items circled in each column.

Analytical	Looks for results	Friendly	Enthusiastic
Fact finder	Change agent	Cooperative	Optimistic
Attention to detail	Action oriented	Steady	Facilitate
Logical	Bottom line	Reliable	Interactive
Need for accuracy	Controlling	Consistent	Creative
Thinker	Set Direction	Helpful	Excitement
Needs a reason	Accomplishes	Loyal	Passionate
Organized thoughts	Goals	Agreeable	Influencer
Data oriented	Self appointed leader	Considers others input	Flexible
Linear processing	Results oriented	Accommodates	New solutions
Rational	Global thinker	Working relationships	Encourage others ideas
Systematic	Decision maker	Willing to compromise	High Energy
T	E	A	M

Team Player Styles Analysis:

Each of us demonstrates a variety of the behaviors listed previously. Most of us are comfortable with a "primary" style, and some of us may even be comfortable in a "secondary" style.

The column with the highest tally score indicates your "primary" style as defined below:

T = Technical
E = Executor
A = Amiable
M = Motivator

Technical—These individuals tend to "know the job", bring rationality to the discussion, and present their viewpoint based on facts.
Executor—These individuals tend to be seen as the dominant drivers behind the team's efforts, focusing on goals and the bottom-line.
Amiable—These team players work hard to reduce conflict between other team members, and bring steadiness and harmony to the team.
Motivator—These team members are the enthusiastic, spontaneous and high-energy cheerleaders for the team. They also lend creativity to the team.

Understanding and having awareness of the individual styles of your team members is important to the interaction, communication and eventual success of your team.

Five Key Elements

In order for teams to succeed we have identified the five key elements which are: **interpersonal relationship**—provide support and challenge, **active reinforcement**—includes desired rewards and accountability for the group, **external relationship**—synergy, having a good relationship with group, **clearly defined purpose**—these elements must serve the organization and the individual which provides focus and direction so teams can move forward and **talented members**—with a full complement of competencies, knowledge and skills, employees require the necessary knowledge and skill set to reach success.

There are advantages and disadvantages to working with teams. Working in teams allows for a variety of viewpoints, pooling of talents, decrease in competition, and more brainpower to generate innovative ideas for thinking out of the box. However, there are disadvantages such as taking longer to make decisions, dealing with more conflicts, individuals giving up personal interest, and being accountable for other team members. Successful teams must allow for individual creativity (for motivation). Creativity is an integral part of the team process. Teams need to be made up of top performers; individuals who are highly committed to the group's success. Teams that want to perform at the synergistic level need to have members who are able to generate random ideas and function in highly creative ways. We are all innately creative as children. A leader needs to permit employees to continue to be creative; that's how teams realize ultimate success.

KEY BEHAVIORS
"Teamwork"

- Encourage participation by all members

- Open minded

- Ask for feedback on team performance

- Request input on goals and objectives

- Convey importance of independent contribution to teamwork

Coaching Your Employees For Success—"Developing Key Talent"

"You've got to do what you do well."

—*Lou Noto, Mobil*

Test Your Knowledge: What Is Coaching?

- What is the value of coaching?

- What is the purpose of coaching?

- How does coaching impact the individual employee?

- How does coaching impact the organization?

- Which employees are likely candidates for coaching?

This chapter will focus on the importance of coaching and the value it brings to the organization. When an organization establishes a meaningful coaching program, a leader as a coach becomes valuable for the employee, which will impact the organization's needs as well as align the organization's objectives and goals.

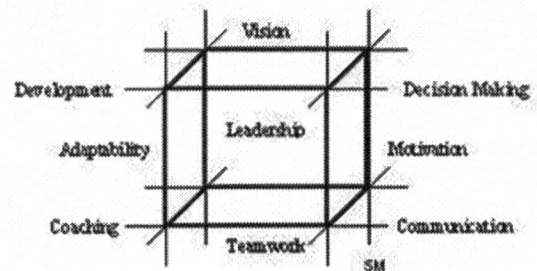

Employees are allowed to learn from mistakes: Ask if it has a serious impact to the organization? Was it the first time or a repeat? Was proper training conducted? Were tools and resources provided? Were expectations clear and set?

Definition of Learning:

Learning has happened when employees can demonstrate newly obtained knowledge and skills.

Coaching has been most visible in sports, not so true in today's corporate culture. Corporate America has embraced the importance and benefits in coaching their high potential employees. Coaching is a valuable element in an employee development program that involves effective communication between an employee and their coach. Organizations need to invest more time and energy in staff development in order to meet future leadership needs. Coaching needs to be an ongoing process in order for it to be embedded in a corporate culture. In order for coaching to be successful, leaders need to commit the time.

Coaching is about assisting solid performers, setting challenging goals and creating career potential. It's not about criticizing performance. Employees do not need to view coaching as a need for poor performance, being genuine is important. Leaders should be eager to create top talent for their organizations. Coaching has become less formal and more immediate than training. Coaching needs to be a lasting contract that focuses on the employee's well-being and interest. The authors stress the importance of giving feedback regularly. A leader and an employee need to go into coaching with the right attitude. Employees are inherently good and they want to contribute and add value to the organization. Employees want to improve themselves. The coaching process allows employees to make mistakes and leaders need to allow the employees to learn from those mistakes.

The leader's job is to understand the employee's role and how it fits in the overall organization. A coach needs to observe employees closely and provide constructive feedback. In the process of coaching, a leader must establish rapport, build and nurture trust, and be approachable, open and authentic. This will make the learning process enjoyable. A leader needs to continue to positively challenge their employees. The intent of coaching is to renew and fine-tune the employee's skills and abilities for their current and future organizational role.

When coaching has been successfully implemented in an organization, it improves communication between employees and leaders. Establishing a positive environment sets the right tone by supplying constructive feedback, which will allow leaders to overcome the challenges in today's corporate environment.

Will You Make A Good Coach?

Coaching your employees is a proven way to develop their skills and improve their performance. Take the initiative to establish a program to coach your best employees. Do not wait to design a program when employees need the assistance. Good employees need coaching and your job as an effective leader is to draw in those opportunities.

The Essentials:

1. **Assurance**—Employees need to open up about their work related concerns and questions. Keep personal information confidential. Discuss issues and concerns openly. Share your personal information when feasible.

2. **Modeling**—Employees will usually work harder for a leader who has improved their own skills (modeling the desired behaviors). Explain your expectations clearly. Reward the behaviors the organization has identified.

3. **Support**—A good coach can alleviate employee stress by praise and encouragement. Ask for their input and demonstrate that you care.

4. **Incentive**—Employees must want this themselves; a coach's responsibility is to find the desire and acknowledge it.

5. **Goal Setting**—A key part of coaching is helping employees decide what they want to do. Assist them and align their goals with the business needs and objective.

6. **Development Plans**—Establish a plan with the employee and create the buy-in that resources will be provided.

Establishing a coaching program will identify employee's strengths and weaknesses in specific skills their organization may require. Skillful coaches are aware that successful coaching can only be achieved by establishing a mutual rewarding partnership. Here are some signs when to coach employees: an employee was given a huge project, and it's a real challenge. You noticed a change in attitude. Employees persistently ask for additional responsibilities.

Becoming A Coach

Directions: In order to coach, coaches need to observe employee's work closely to have meaningful substantive feedback to assist "coachee's". Follow the steps mentioned below.

- Identify a situation that may require guidance (it may be professional development).
- Identify an individual that will be able to benefit from coaching.
- Open first meeting with details and purpose.
- Identify situations that will increase knowledge or skills on projects, dealing with conflict, improving communication skills or decision-making abilities.
- Establish a partnership and frequent meeting schedule and gain commitment from the early start.
- Have topics for discussion a week prior to scheduled meetings.

The Value Of Mentoring

"We must open the doors of opportunity, but we must also equip our people to walk through those doors."

—Lyndon B. Johnson

Many Forms

Mentoring has many faces. The practice of mentoring can present itself through formal programs, informal relationships or peer group conversations. Mentoring also serves different purposes. The most recognizable of these are described in the following text.

New Employee Programs

Traditionally referred to as "transitional mentoring", this mentoring assists new employees in becoming acclimated to the culture of the department and any peculiarities of the environment in which the job operates. Direct benefits of transitional mentoring include:

- Get employees focused and productive.

- Transitional mentoring opens lines of communication, not only with the employee and their direct supervisor, but also with peers and other subject matter experts. This communication is generally focused on the job tasks and may include on-the-job training.

- Align new employees to the organization's priorities and culture.

- Open communications also serve to provide the new employee with the "low-down" on organizational goals and priorities, who to talk to for answers, and quirks about do's and don'ts in the department.

- Gain commitment to the department's goals and strategies.

- Conversations with peers can help to build a sense of belonging. Employees who buy into this "community" environment are much more likely to support the goals of the organization and commit to the priorities and cultural perspectives.

Develop Specialized Skills

Sometimes known as "Navigational Mentoring", this focuses on an employee's personal and professional development. This type of mentoring can cover a wide gambit of objectives, as the mentoring relationship is designed to focus on practically any topic the employee desires. Frequently this will present itself as skill building for a future job, perfecting skills for a current job, or building a network of contacts for the future. Side effects of Navigational Mentoring include:

- Communicating the organizational culture.

- Conversations with a mentor can help an employee understand "how it's done here". Many employees struggle to understand why things are the way they are, and benefit greatly from insights a mentor can provide. This information greatly enhances the employee's effectiveness within the organization, and leads to greater productivity and retention.

- Career path.

- Growth planning can be vastly amplified through the mentoring process. An experienced mentor can help the protégé flush out the details of future career goals, and assist the protégé to realize the skill sets required to achieve their goals.

Develop Bench Strength

The third form of mentoring focuses on developing the organizations internal talent pool. This helps ensure organizational sustainability through a body of employees who understand the culture in which they operate. Related strategies include the use of organizational inventories, succession planning, and leadership development processes to ensure that the employees who will be driving operations in the future have the appropriate skill sets and can operate under the desired philosophical model.

Benefits

Organization

The organization realizes many benefits from the mentoring process. More obvious on the list are:

- Improves employee retention.

- Strengthens the organization.

- Shared information and knowledge.

- Competitive advantage in the "war for talent."

- Enhances morale.

Mentor

Benefits to the mentor focusing on demonstrated ability and opportunities to develop themselves. In addition, the mentoring relationship may give the mentor a rare opportunity to see into other functions or parts of the organization.

Enhances advancement prospects by giving the mentor the opportunity to demonstrate:

- Efforts toward improving interpersonal and management skills.
- Understanding of tolerance for different types of people.
- Ability to solve problems.
- Ability to identify and respond to the needs of other people.
- Willingness to take responsibility and help others.
- Ability to set goals and priorities.
- Ability to maintain working relationships.
- Motivation to help grow the organization.
- Renews the feeling that "tenured" employees are valued.

Protégé

The protégé generally finds great benefit in the mentoring process, especially when the protégé is the focal point of the process. No matter what type of mentoring is being conducted, the protégé is in a position to grow and develop. Much of this is based on the assumption that the protégé is interested in the process. Many of the benefits have already been discussed, so the following list serves to recap previous discussions:

- Receives honest and impartial feedback.
- Understands career path requirements.
- Demonstrates understanding of own strengths and weaknesses.
- Develops skills for current or future jobs.

Limitations

These mentoring processes are not the cure-all for any organization. The amount of benefit the organization receives is directly correlated to the knowledge and skill level of the mentors and protégés, and to the culture of the organization. Different organizations will experience varying levels of success based on the acceptance of the process and the operational environment. Program requirements and guidelines may need to be modified in order for the organization to realize a return on investment. The list below represents a sample of program points to be considered:

- The program must be flexible enough to accommodate personality clashes and workload demands.
- Goals must be clearly stated.
- The time frame needs to be specified.

Coaching vs. Mentoring

A lot of confusion exists regarding the differences in coaching and mentoring.

Coaching

- Coaching is a process that enables learning and development to occur and thus performance to improve.
- Focuses on helping employees work through problems.
- Dealing with business challenges.
- Uses questioning techniques to facilitate the coachee's own thought processes in order to identify solutions and actions rather than take a wholly directive approach.
- The coach generally has significant experience in the coachee's situation, but relies on their ability to question.

Mentoring

- Goal or development-based process.
- Applies tools and techniques that may include training, facilitating, counseling and networking.
- Mentoring is off-line help by one person to another in making significant transitions in knowledge, work or thinking.
- Mentors generally have significant experience in the protégés area of focus.

- A mentor is an experienced and trusted coach who can help a protégé learn new skills, sharpen current skills, and guide them in learning and development.

Coaching in the workplace can benefit promotional opportunities, team development, leadership development, succession planning and performance improvement which renovates the corporate culture.

"Are you green and growing or ripe and rotting."

—Ray Kroc, Founder, McDonalds

KEY BEHAVIORS
"Coaching"

- Demonstrate effective behaviors and traits

- Inspire others

- Great story teller

- Challenge the person's potential

- Develop a partnership with employees

- Fair and objective

Adaptability—"Dealing With Change"

Test Your Knowledge: What Is Adaptability?

- Are you receptive and open to trying something new, even if things are going well?

- Are you stuck in the "*this is the way we've always done it*" mentality?

- Do your employees see change as a bottleneck or barrier?

- To what extent do you allow employees to participate in the change process?

- What causes employees' resistance to change?

Dealing with change requires a clear vision, an understanding of your current culture and the ability to make decisions.

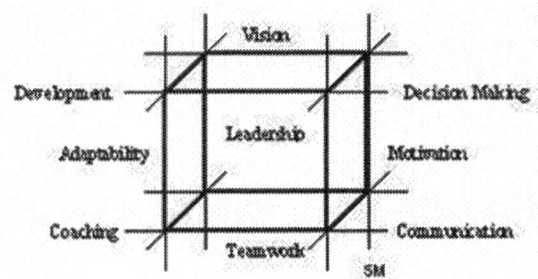

Change is inevitable; corporations are continuously striving to improve their organizations. Leaders are responsible for instituting organizational change. These leaders need to model change and maintain a level of comfort for their employees. For some, change is a difficult process and others see it as an opportunity.

A basic definition of *organizational change* is redesigning the fundamental organization and rethinking organizational processes and strategies to achieve dramatic performance improvement measured in the following areas: profit, quality, service and speed.

For organizational change effort to become successful, leadership needs to clearly communicate those changes as soon as it is appropriate?

Communication may include all employee meetings (town hall meeting), written communication, and department staff meetings. The best approach would be to utilize a blended selection in order to reach your entire workforce. In some circumstances change does get implemented to the current corporate culture or any built in barriers the organization may have.

Society and humanity are making these demands for change. This is why we have identified adaptability as a core trait of effective leaders. We stress in today's climate and environment that leaders become flexible and patient in order to become effective in today's organizations. One of the challenges is helping employees break free from the way business is run today. Stagnant and constant change causes chaos and unproductive employees. With uncertainty in the organization, their respective roles and the viability of this change effort causes doubt. Some may feel there have been many similar attempts that have failed and wonder what will be different this time. Organizations will not survive if leaders do not institutionalize the changes. The change process will generate innovative ideas for the same old problems. This will be true if leaders keep an open mind because their role will be convincing others this is the right thing to do.

The Four A's Of Adaptability
(Simplifying the Cycle of Change)

Stage One: Astonishment

Employees here have been comfortable. The employee is surprised that a change is happening. In this stage the employee has disagreements about the change. Some reactions may include dissent and increase in rumors. Thoughts include, "I can't believe this is really happening to me."

Stage Two: Abandonment

Employees become very negative; anger sets in because of the uncertainty of this change, which is causing fear, not knowing how this will affect their livelihood. Employees start to question why now, "What will happen to me?"

Stage Three: Accommodating

Employees start identifying with the positive affects of the change. After some period of time (after their initial reaction) the employees realize the change has taken place, and take the opportunity to become part of the process rather than continue to be an adversary. At this point employees feel, "This wasn't that bad."

Stage Four: Acceptance

Employees in this stage have completely accepted the change. The new process has become part of their life. Employees no longer are uncomfortable or resistant to the change. Employees start to say, "This was the right thing to do."

In today's rapidly moving global economy, if leaders do not recognize the need for change by answering the questions below, reaching their goals and the organization's goals will not become a reality. Leadership is needed to identify change as well as motivate people to change their behaviors.

What's the reason for change? What are we doing this for? Why is change a priority now? What challenges will we be facing? What will this change mean to me?

In changing times, the most important behavioral trait is adaptability, the willingness to do something different which may not have been your idea or suggestion. Leaders need to invent new ways of doing things, which allows employees to participate in the process. As we stated, employees want to be part of the process so they can add value to the organization and feel as if they are truly part of this high performance team.

In order for adaptability in the workplace, we have identified these key elements for success:

- Communication
- Address employee concerns
- Establish a positive environment
- Promote employee involvement
- Embrace change—ongoing

Change for successful organizations is difficult because they are so successful and profitable. Why change something that is doing so well? One thing we can count on is change is constant. Depending on the size of your organization, it takes three to five years to embrace change. We continuously have to remind ourselves that we need to be adaptable. Despite all efforts, adaptability is challenging because it's different, new, and more work. It takes more time, is more stressful and it's overwhelming. We must adapt to change quickly. It's important to remember change equals opportunity.

"Never look at the doors closing behind you or you'll miss the ones opening ahead."

—Cyril Magnin, Chair, Joseph Magnin

KEY BEHAVIORS
"Adaptability"

- Positive thinking

- Flexible

- Maintain focus

- Comfortable with ambiguity

- Remains strong in uncertain times

- Recognizes opportunity

- Demonstrates effective listening skills

Development—"Growing The Right Talent"

"Your success depends on the success of the people around you."

—*Benjamin H. Bristol*

Test Your Knowledge: What Is Development?

- What is development?

- Who is responsible for development?

- What does development look like? How is it structured?

- How can progress be monitored?

- What is the value of development to the organization?

We end the leadership framework model by linking development for both leaders and employees to the organization's vision and goals, which leads to the path of success.

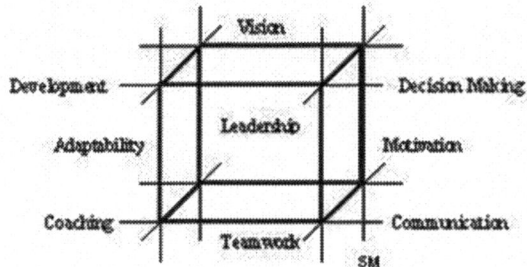

Employee Development

Leaders must be willing to help employees learn and develop additional abilities and skills. Buy-in and commitments made to one's growth with the organization helps create that high performing organization that we are all committed to create as leaders. Commitment to one's personal growth and potential opportunities within an organization allows the employees to have a sense of belonging and the feeling that their talent contributes, which in return adds value to the overall business strategy. With leaders recognizing employee needs and interest, the corporate culture of creating a high performing organization will be strengthened. If employees are asked to take on new responsibilities they need to be given the proper training and resources to become competent and successful in their new role.

Leaders need to identify and create a learning environment that will match the developmental goals and corporate objectives with the individual's interest in mind, making sure the employee understands the relevance of their development and that the leader furnishes essential resources to assist the employee. Employees need to manage their development path to achieve success. A successful leader must first determine what type of learning issues their employees are facing and stress the importance of establishing a development plan. As plans are put in place, establish an ongoing evaluation process for employees to provide the appropriate coaching and feedback required. A leader should decide with the employee whether their objectives align with the corporate vision and business goals. This would build a sense of ownership in the employee development plan.

"Ability will never catch up with the demand for it".

—*Malcolm Forbes, Publisher, Forbes*

In this process of planning, leaders need to sit down with the employee and discuss where the employee wants to be and then provide guidance to develop the best plan. A key insight a leader needs to provide for the employee is structure, which is the best avenue to reach their goals. A leader becomes a sounding board and provides reality checks in the direction the employee wishes to go. Development plans should be reviewed annually to ensure employee interest and alignment of organization objectives.

Do leaders measure and track employee development progress? Leaders need to assist employees in their development plans. Ownership still falls on the employee's shoulder. A leader needs to create that alliance between the development needs of an employee and the overall business strategy of the organization. The process includes having one on one's with their employees. Being able to provide constructive feedback is a critical component of an employee's development plan. Leaders must be able to match individual skill sets to a specific job function.

Leadership Development

Leadership development should consist of feedback (use of a multi-rater), development plans, coaching, the opportunity to experience a broader range of decision-making, new assignments, and people interaction. In addition to training programs (generally beneficial to gain new skills) experiential learning activities create a positive and practical outcome.

Experiential learning on a large-scale basis fosters an ideal leadership culture to drive the organization to high performance.

The practice of sharing information gained from training or experience is invaluable. This approach saves corporate resources and spreads the knowledge while creating a common language.

Is It Worth It?

1. Pick one behavior at which you can improve, that will make a positive difference at work or in your life. *Note*: Each team member picks one item and stays with item for this activity.

2. Go around the table and share the behaviors identified.

3. Share the benefits for each improvement.

Analyzing Development

Steps to identify development needs:

Leader Roles
What are the organization's goals and objectives?
What are the organization's training needs?
Is there an alignment or natural fit for the employee's skills?

Employee Roles
Establish an employee development plan.
Gain buy-in and commitment from leadership.

Development Activity

This activity will identify the knowledge and skills possessed by your team. It is important to recognize both the strengths of your team as well as skills that need development.

Instructions:

Ensure each participant has paper and pen.

1. Individually, name 3 strengths you bring to the team.

Strengths
1.
2.
3.

2. Record responses from each individual on a flipchart.
3. Categorize all responses (i.e. organize like-strengths together and identify relevant themes).
4. Identify the strengths (themes) that support the groups' vision and drive toward achieving business results.
5. Identify critical skill gaps that will lead to achieving results.
6. Build a plan to close the gaps (i.e. developing skills in current staff, hiring personnel with skills, etc.)

Leadership Assessment

Directions: Rate yourself for each of the following statements using the scale below. Keep in mind there are no right answers.

5 - highly characteristic of my style
4 – characteristic of my style
3 – somewhat characteristic of my style
2 – uncharacteristic of my style
1 – highly uncharacteristic of my style

	Statements	Rating
1.	I provide information to employees at all times through various avenues.	
2.	I offer support and guidance for all my employees.	
3.	I am receptive and open to trying something new.	
4.	I create value by energizing my employees.	
5.	I establish clear goals for myself.	
6.	I support new solutions and innovation.	
7.	I clearly communicate the company vision at all levels.	
8.	I effectively lead the organization through rapid change.	
9.	I continue to develop myself as well as others.	
10	I have a proven track record making sound decisions in the course of my career.	
11	I have established high performance teams in my organization.	
12	I am very confident in my decision-making abilities, rarely second guessing myself.	
13	I believe in coaching all employees, regardless of performance level.	
14	I am a great believer in inspiring employees.	
15	I endorse and encourage participation from all my employees.	
16	I clearly understand the purpose of this organization.	
17	I find others trust my decision-making skills.	
18	I continue to grow key talent and future leaders.	
19	I regularly praise my employees for a job well done.	
20	I believe I've improved employee performance through coaching.	
21	I trust in the importance of establishing developmental opportunities.	
22	I foster a teamwork environment.	
23	I clearly and regularly communicate expectations with my staff.	
24	I can picture where I would like to take this organization.	

Leadership Assessment Scoring

	Vision		Decision Making		Motivation		Communication
Question							
5		10		4		1	
16		12		14		7	
24		17		19		23	
Total							
	Teamwork		Coaching		Adaptability		Development
Question							
11		2		3		9	
15		13		6		18	
22		20		8		21	
Total							

Copy the scores from the previous page in the blanks above to compute your leadership score. The traits with the highest totals are your area of strengths. The area(s) with a low score are the suggested traits for improvement. These are the areas of opportunity. We encourage further development in these areas. If your very balanced among the traits, select the trait(s) you would like to develop further.

KEY BEHAVIORS
"Development"

- Make development a priority

- Provide opportunity

- Make training available

- Provide feedback mechanisms

- Show interest in employees future

- Follow through

- Analyze development needs

Organizational Culture—"Defining The Intangible"

"There is something that is much more scarce, something rarer than ability, it is the ability to recognize ability."

—Robert Half, Personnel Agency Executive

Test Your Knowledge: What Is Culture?

- Are your values and beliefs in line with the organization?

- How do your employees know what behaviors are acceptable?

- What are the "unwritten rules" in your organization?

- Is there visible evidence of your organization's culture?

- How does your organization's culture impact employees?

Often leaders believe that "organizational culture" is some nebulous and intangible phenomenon that can't be touched because you can't see it. In reality, you can touch culture. We often don't see it because we choose not to look!

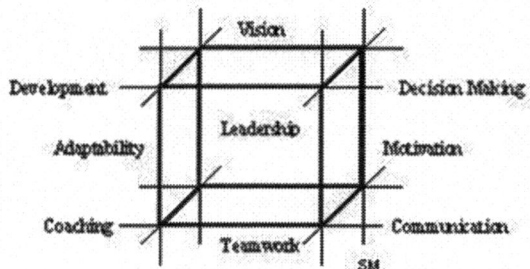

Culture affects every component of the organization, from compensation practices and leadership to operational strategies and the work environment. Any attempt to change the organization without first understanding the culture can end up futile and frustrating. However, to understand the culture, you must be prepared to look deeply into yourself and your organization. Often this will result in extreme discomfort as you uncover cultural evidence that is not in line with your personal values and beliefs.

Levels Within The Culture

To clearly look at the organizational culture, you have to understand the composition of the culture. Like an onion, culture can be described in terms of its layers.

What do the levels indicate?

On The Surface

From the outside, an onion may appear very different. You can find white, yellow or purple onions, small, medium or large onions. These surface level descriptors, commonly referred to as "artifacts", are the bane of many change efforts because leaders tend to hang teamwork posters on the wall and then proceed to describe their culture as one that supports team concepts. The outer layer of our organizational onion generally represents the things we see, hear and feel when you walk into the organization. Examples of the surface layer can be understood by examining:

- What do you see?
- What do you hear people say?
- What do you feel when you walk through the building?

- How is the property decorated?
- What is the climate based on how people behave?
- What are your emotional reactions?
- Dress codes
- Level of formality in authority relationships
- Working hours
- Meetings
- Decision making processes
- Social events
- Jargon, identity symbols
- Rites and rituals
- How is conflict handled?
- Work/Life balance

Digging Deeper Into The Organization

To get a more accurate sense of what the culture looks like and the implications that organizational culture can have on the rest of the organization; you have to ask the questions that will help peel back the layers of this onion.

Espoused Values

Several experts on organizational culture have adopted this term "espoused theory" or "espoused values" to describe the phenomenon that occurs when an individual or an organization publicly adopts a practice or value, but does not integrate it into the culture. We frequently see this in teamwork, where people hang posters (surface level "artifacts") on the wall and openly support teamwork, but fail to build an incentive program to reinforce the team concept. To understand the middle layer ask:

- What does the organization "value"? How do they show it?
- Why do they do the things they do? (i.e. Why do they construct office areas the way they do?)

What Works

We are often inclined to find a quick method to examine the culture (looking for quick fixes may be part of the organizations culture!). "Culture Surveys" are quite common, but fail to dig deep enough into the onion to get the valuable insight into the corporate culture. These surveys tend to produce results that describe only the outer layers of your onion. After all, culture cannot be sufficiently described on a scale of 1 to 5.

The Interview Process

More effectively, focus groups and interviews can help clearly describe all layers of the culture. Asking a group to describe the organization, its reason for being and how it has evolved takes you to the heart of the organization's culture, and helps you understand how you can work within the culture, or what changes are needed to create a sustainable organization in the future.

Sample Interview

Underlying Assumptions (Digging real deep)
(How does this aid or hinder employees in accomplishing goals?)

Thinking Historically

What beliefs or values are taken for granted?
What are those things that are defined as "that's just how we do it here"?
What is the mission of the organization?
What justifies its reason for being?
How does the organization's strategy and goals fit the mission?
Where did this strategy come from? What is it based on?

Today

How and why did the organization develop the structure in place today?
Does the structure and design of how work gets done reflect the beliefs of leadership?
Are there subcultures present within the organization?
What are the error detection systems in the organization?
What happens if it is discovered that important goals are not being met?
What are the "badges of membership" in the organization?

Are there special symbols or privileges to symbolize membership? Degrees of membership?

How do you define who is an insider vs. outsider?

What does it mean to be late or early? What does it mean to come in early or leave early?

Do meetings start on time? Do they end on time?

How is rank reflected physically or spatially?

Does the physical layout reflect working style and status?

Human Implications

What might be the people implications?

Do you have the right people?

Do they have the right skills?

Does the organization have the right environment?

What does the environment look like?

What is the implication on compensation?

Are there policy implications?

What incentives have been put in place?

What does this mean to the people?

Closing Thoughts

"Winners can tell you where they are going, what they plan to do along the way and who will be sharing the adventure with them."

—*Denis Waitley, Motivational Speaker and Author*

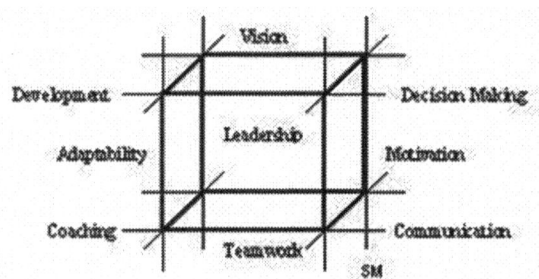

This T.E.A.M.WORKS[SM] Leadership Model displays innovation and authorizes the leader to think outside the box. The eight key traits we have presented will foster an effective leader that organizations require today. The model represents the essential blueprint to build effective leadership.

In some cases employees need to be told what to do and leaders need to find out what motivates them and let them do it. We can't stress enough the importance of demonstrating your confidence in your employees' abilities. Let the employees perform what they do best, and develop them where it makes sense. Your ultimate goal is to be able to reach peak performance for yourself and your team. By creating a sense of direction or vision, your team will understand the path required to carry out its mission. Once the vision is in place, you can make effective decisions and tap into employees' potential to create a high trust organization.

You'll be a better leader if you're not the only leader on your team. To enlighten and empower your entire workforce you need to spend the time developing each team member's potential. Vision, decision-making, motivation, communication, teamwork, coaching, adaptability and development are all key traits of effective leadership. Leaders convey their confidence in their employees' abilities and needs. Start by recognizing and rewarding model behaviors. Encourage all team members to recognize each other's accomplishments. Leaders need to give employees the tools and resources to become that successful high performing employee.

Don't limit coaching to a handful of poor-performing employees; premier performers also need the benefit of your feedback, encouragement and support. Remember that coaching isn't just about criticizing performance (we refer to this as constructive feedback or areas of opportunities). Use your coaching sessions to help solid workers set challenging goals, discuss their career potential and ask for their input on the job role and workplace procedures. Keep communication positive; upbeat and motivational. Leaders often fail to understand the relationship between employee motivation and reward systems.

In order for leaders to make successful choices and decisions, leaders need to foster an open climate of discussion. Leaders need to approach change with an open mind. Involve everyone by assigning him or her to a role in the organization so the employee(s) feel they are adding value to the bottom line. A leader needs to assist the employee in finding their place in the organization. Leaders also need to identify the skills that are lacking from the organization. Training employees is the first step in developing needed skills and the desirable behaviors (culture) that leaders are trying to create. Organizations can't afford to say that they cannot invest in workforce development. Today's leader must have the essential interpersonal skills of effective communication, active listening, influencing and decision-making.

In order to be effective, they need to adapt their behavior to maximize performance by improving interpersonal relationships with their employees. Leaders need to establish a culture of cooperation. It's crucial to diagnose problems correctly before any decision can be made. Start by identifying and defining the issue and it's boundaries clearly. We can't stress enough the importance of setting clear expectations and goals.

Leadership is everyone's business; when achieved it benefits ourselves, our team and the organization. Leaders need to create that productive and sometimes fun work environment (there is nothing wrong with having a little fun at work) and increase morale for their organization. Make every effort to leverage employee's involvement and participation, and demonstrate the importance that everyone counts and needs to be heard. Establishing trust and encouraging two-way communication will allow employees to feel ownership in their respective organization. A critical leader role is to create an alignment with employees to meet customer and organizational expectations.

We have witnessed that managers can transform the attitudes and behavior of their employees by altering their mindset. Allow employees time to see the need for change, and absorb that change and eventually agree with and support it. The authors stress the need for change agents at all levels of an organization. Employees need to see people they respect modeling that "new behavior". When employees believe in the needed change, they will adapt their behavior for the well being of their organization because their contributions add value to the organization—that's what motivates people in a high performance organization.

Leaders that behave ethically are more likely to develop a culture that employees and customers would want to be associated with; it takes more than just establishing the words of a formal ethics program. You need to ask how your decisions align with your own personal values and beliefs. Would you want this decision happening to you? Leaders need to be accountable for their decisions, ask how fair it was and reflect whether or not it was the right decision.

You now have the framework for developing effective leaders within your organization. Use the tools and resources found in this book to build the culture and organization that reflects what your organization stands for.

"A leader is someone who can take a group of people to a place they don't think they can go."

—Bob Eaton

Index

A
Adaptability 8

C
Coaching 8, 9, 50, 51, 57
Communication 7, 33, 34, 38, 40, 63

D
Decision Making 7
Development 8

I
Innovation 8

L
Leadership Model 5

M
Motivation 7, 26, 56

R
relationship 2, 3, 7, 26, 39, 40, 47, 54, 56

T
Teamwork 8
traits 3, 6, 9

V
Vision 7, 11, 12

0-595-33592-6

www.ingramcontent.com/pod-product-compliance
Lightning Source LLC
Chambersburg PA
CBHW030904180526
45163CB00004B/1692